ALL JOBS ARE IMPORTANT

TODOS LOS TRABAJOS SON IMPORTANTES

Alejandra Vinasco

wordeee
where words connect

ALL JOBS ARE IMPORTANT

TODOS LOS TRABAJOS SON IMPORTANTES

All Jobs Are Important
Todos Los Trabajos Son Importantes

First edition

ISBN (Paperback): 978-1-959811-00-8
ISBN (e-book): 978-1-959811-01-5

Library of Congress Control Number: 2022920117

Spanish Translation: Gustavo A. González

Cover and Interior Design: Amit Dey

Illustrations: Amita Rathore

Website: www.wordeee.com
Twitter: wordeeeupdates
Facebook: facebook.com/wordeee/
e-mail: contact@wordeee.com

Published by Wordeee in the United States, Beacon, New York 2022

Printed in USA

It all started...

Todo comenzó...

...when my family and I unexpectedly moved to the United States from Colombia, South America. My mother explained that we were moving to this strange new place because my father was going to be starting a brand new job there. Soon after we moved, my dad lost his new job.

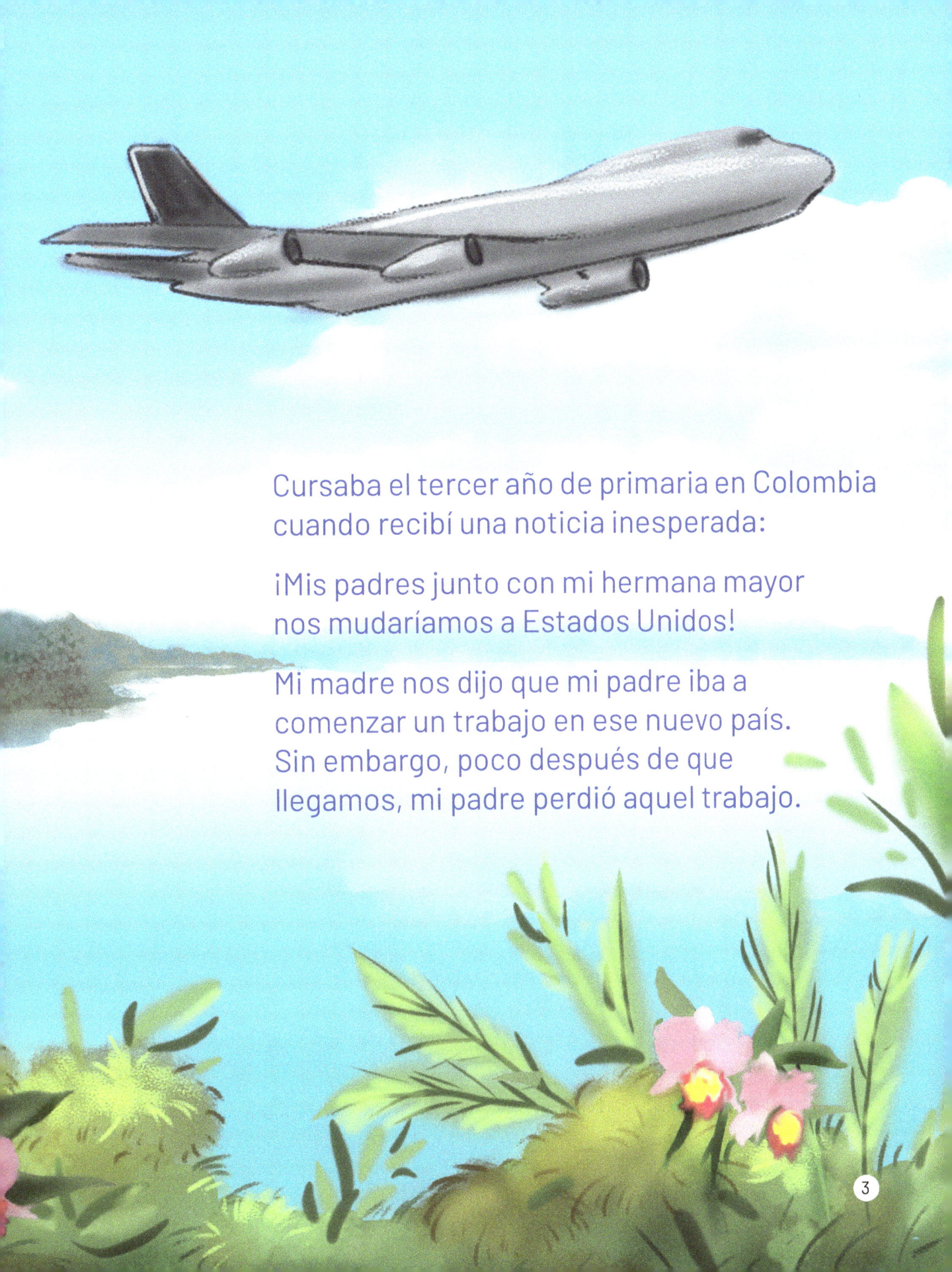

Cursaba el tercer año de primaria en Colombia cuando recibí una noticia inesperada:

¡Mis padres junto con mi hermana mayor nos mudaríamos a Estados Unidos!

Mi madre nos dijo que mi padre iba a comenzar un trabajo en ese nuevo país. Sin embargo, poco después de que llegamos, mi padre perdió aquel trabajo.

After losing his new job, my dad made the decision to use the last bit of the money he had saved up to start his own landscaping company. He began to work outside under the scorching, hot sun, mowing grass and planting flowers almost every day of the week.

Entonces, él decidió usar el último dinero que tenía para lanzar su propia compañía de jardinería. Así fue como comenzó a cortar grama y plantar flores casi todos los días bajo un sol abrasador.

My mother could not find a job as a nurse because she did not speak English. She finally found a job installing wallpaper in vacant apartments and houses.

She would take me to work with her almost every Saturday and Sunday. I would help her pick up the old scraps of wall paper from the floor while she hung the new, colorful wallpaper on plain white walls.

Entre tanto, mi madre no podía conseguir empleo como enfermera porque no hablaba inglés hasta que, finalmente encontró un trabajo para instalar papel tapiz.

Recuerdo que todos los fines de semana me llevaba a las casas donde hacía su trabajo, y mientras ella pegaba los rollos de papel en las paredes, yo le ayudaba a recoger los sobrantes del suelo.

I did not always enjoy going to work with my mama but I knew how important it was for me to help her.

On my way back home from work, I would always wonder if other kids ever got to go to work with their parents. If they did, what types of jobs did their parents have and what was it like?

No siempre disfrutaba trabajar junto a mi mamá, pero sabía cuán importante era ayudarle. A menudo, en nuestro recorrido de vuelta a casa me veía en otros escenarios y me preguntaba si acaso otros niños tenían que ir a trabajar juntos a sus padres.

Si lo hacían, ¿qué tipo de trabajos tenían esos padres? ¿Y cómo sería aquello?

I was curious to know how much fun it would be to go out in space with your dad or mom if they were astronauts.

Entonces imaginaba qué divertido sería ir al espacio con un papá o una mamá si ellos fueran astronautas.

I wondered too, what it would be like to go to the hospital and help your mom or dad take care of sick or injured patients if they were a nurses?

O en el caso de que fueran enférmeros, ¿cómo sería ir con ellos a un hospital para ayudar a sanar heridos o gente enferma?

Would you be able to fit and ride with your dad or mom in the mail cart if they were mail carriers? How many mailboxes would you have the privilege to help them open?

Si fueran carteros, ¿podría caber en el carrito del correo y andar con ellos para ayudarles a repartir cartas y paquetes? ¿Cuántos buzones tendría el privilegio de abrir?

Could your fingers become as strong as your business mom or business dad's fingers if you typed on the keyboard and clicked on the mouse like they did all day?

También pensaba, ¿será que con teclear y manejar una computadora todo el día, todos los días tus dedos podrían llegar a ser tan fuertes como los dedos de sus padres?

How big a hole would your dad or mom have to drill if they were construction workers and had to fix or make a road?

Y si fueran obreros, ¿qué tan grande sería el hueco que mi padre o mi madre tendrían que hacer para arreglar una calle?

I also wondered about whose cat you would help your firefighting dad or mom rescue? If you helped them get a kitten down from a tree, and the kitten did not have an owner, would you be able to adopt the kitten?

Incluso me preguntaba, ¿qué gato ayudaría a rescatar si mis padres fueron bomberos? Y si ayudarse a rescatar un gatito de un árbol y el animalito no tuviera dueño, ¿podría adoptarlo?

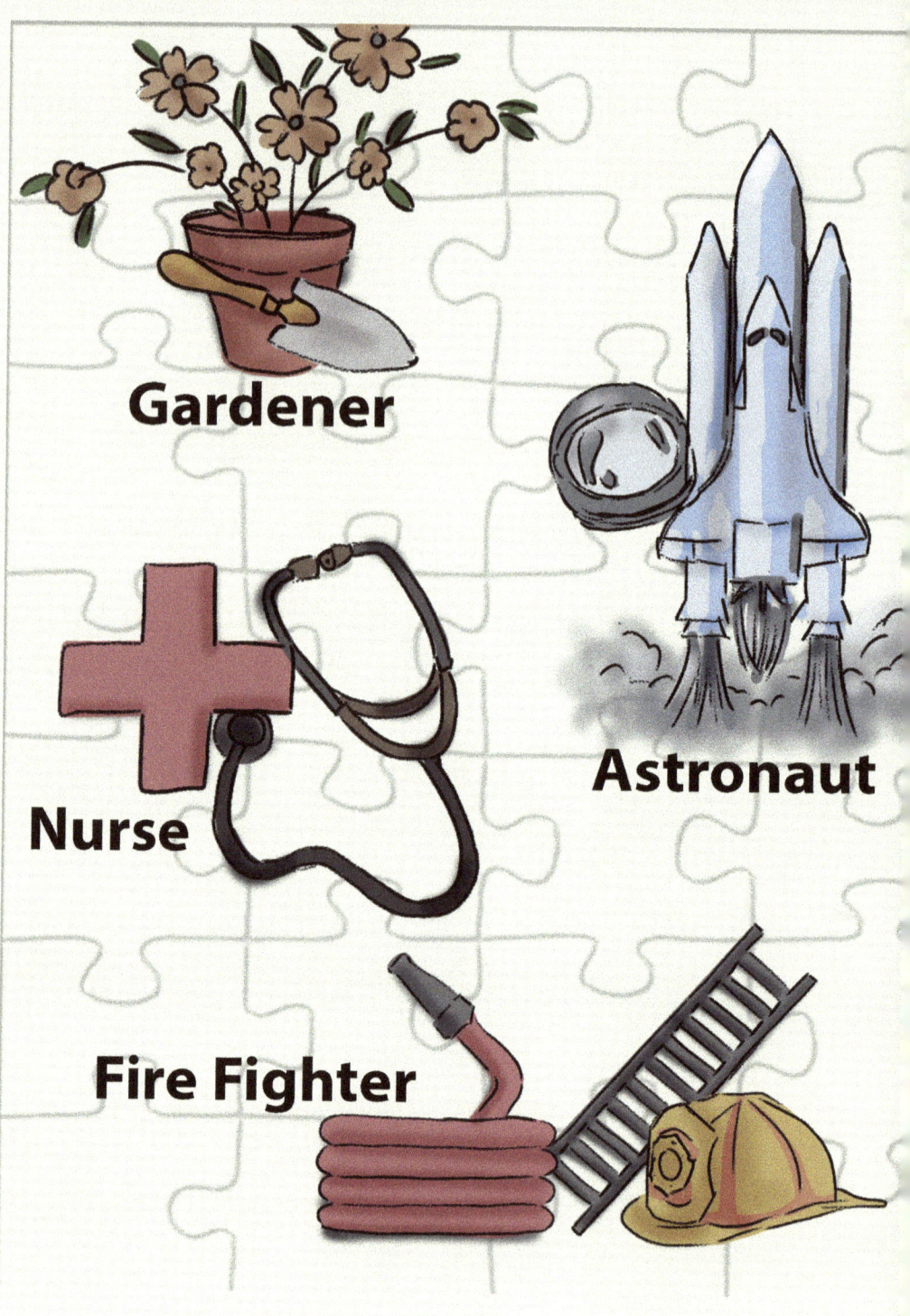

Gardener

Astronaut

Nurse

Fire Fighter

There are many different and important jobs that parents
have. Sometimes our parents or family members lose
their jobs. Other times you have to move away because
they got a new job. I know that all jobs involve helping
22   another person and that is why I cannot make up my mind

Office Worker

Mail Carrier

Wallpaper Installer

Construction Worker

what job I would like to have when I grow up. I am sure that whatever job you or I end up choosing will be as important as a landscaper, wallpaper installer, astronaut, nurse, mail carrier, business representative, construction worker and fire fighter.

23

jardinero

astronauta

enfermero

bombero

Los padres tienen diferentes trabajos y todos son importantes. A veces nuestros padres o familiares pierden sus trabajos. También ocurre que debes mudarte a otro lugar porque ellos consiguen un nuevo empleo.

Cuando era pequeña entendí que todos los trabajos implicaban ayudar a otras personas, y por eso no lograba

representante de negocios

cartero

decorador/instalador

obrero

decidir qué trabajo me gustaría tener cuando fuera grande.

Sin embargo, hoy puedo decir que cualquier trabajo que escojas será tan importante como el de jardinero, decorador, instalador, astronauta, enfermero, cartero, representante de negocios, obrero o bombero.

AUTHOR'S NOTE

When I was in third grade I moved to the United States with my mom, dad and sister. I had a difficult time making friends at school because I was not able to relate to my peers. Most of my classmates' parents had regular jobs such as mail carriers and nurses. My parent's jobs were different and I felt embarrassed about their occupations. I wrote this book with the intention to create a more understanding environment in the classroom for children from a very young age: kindergarten and up. It is very important that students do not feel ashamed of their parent's occupation and that they don't hold themselves back from pursuing a particular job because of their gender. This book can assist in building acceptance of one another by showing that All Jobs Are Important. It also makes clear that men and women are both capable of doing the same jobs. The main goal of this book is to enlighten students that all jobs serve the same purpose which is to help others. It could also inspire them to be whoever they want to be when they grow up.

NOTA DE LA AUTORA

La experiencia que tuve de pequeña me impulsó a escribir este libro con la intención de ayudar a crear un ambiente de entendimiento acerca del trabajo a partir el jardín de infancia. Es importante que los estudiantes no se sientan avergonzados por la ocupación de sus padres y que no se detengan en la búsqueda de un trabajo en particular.

Este libro busca fomentar la aceptación entre las personas acerca de la importancia de cada trabajo. También sirve para destacar el hecho de que hombres y mujeres son capaces de realizar los mismos trabajos.

En resumen de propósito de este libro es alentar a los estudiantes a que comprendan que todos los trabajos tienen mismo propósito, el cual es servir a los demás e inspirar a los pequeños a que elijan una profesión cuando sean grandes, cualquiera que esta sea.

www.ingramcontent.com/pod-product-compliance
Lightning Source LLC
Chambersburg PA
CBHW041529120626
46551CB00018B/2623